The Cacophony of a Solitary Fool

Dhavnish Shukla

BookLeaf Publishing

Presentation by *BookLeaf Publishing*

Web: www.bookleafpub.com

E-mail: info@bookleafpub.com

ISBN: 9789357445603

First edition 2021

DEDICATION

Dedicated to Krishna and the spirit of understanding

ACKNOWLEDGE MENT

Well, I could probably write another book if I were to thank every person who contributed. Mainly because this book is a collection of poems that were not written in one day or even a year. It is reflective of my perspectives and experiences from different times in my life. Hence, there are a lot of people who helped shape my perspective. But in the strictest spirit of acknowledgement, there are a few I would want to name. My parents have been the ones who planted the seed. My mom has been a true source of strength and hope while my dad is the one who exposed me to the habit of looking deeper. Roma is an expression and a feeling more than a person. Technically, she is my wife but then she is nothing less of inspiration, not only for writing but also to look at the brighter side of life. Special thanks to my new extended family, my in-laws parents for always encouraging me and my brother - Manan to be patient to listen to my poems by taking out time from his gaming sessions. Manjula ma'am the one who ignited the spark of poetry in me by showing me how beautiful poetry is. Cannot forget to thank my almost blood brothers Kush and Dhrupad for always having my back and clapping at my shittiest poems. I can remember how my dear Pravar cheered me up since the time he started recognising faces, and am rarely afraid to fail because I know my uncle Chetan has my back. Nor can I forget the endless support by a few friends who stuck by me through the worst times - Ankit, Riten, Priyal, Medhavini, Dakshata and Dhaval. They have been through a lot, first by listening to my "philosophy", and then by listening to a long poem about it. I will be honest - there are a lot more names I want to write. But these are the names who have endured the longest and the most painful stage of my evolution as a poet. I'd like to thank my mentors at different stages who helped me shape overall as a person without whom I wouldn't be who I am.

PREFACE

Have you ever experienced this? - every time someone falls short of their promise or fail to help you, they have “circumstances” that prevented them from doing so. But when you fail to be helpful to someone, your circumstances are “excuses”. If yes, you are not the only person. But the interesting thing is, even your friend would say the same about you. Who then is right, or wrong? Let me do you a better one, aren’t we all hypocrites? The (not so) bitter truth of human existence is the sub-conscious narcissistic need to survive by exploiting whatever and whoever possible. You don’t think you are that bad, huh? Let me share with you a perspective using an unpopular example. Say you have a friend you are ready to die for. Is your love, your sense of being loyal and helpful because they are “your FRIEND”, or is it because they are “YOUR friend”? The same goes with parents, kids, siblings and humans at large. So many identities – my country, my religion, my gender, race, ethnicity, region, language, city, town, village, family, likes, dislikes, extrovert, introvert, the list just goes on. I am ready to be bigger than myself, sacrifice or even die for what is MINE. Food, clothing and shelter ensure physical survival, which even other living beings do. Humans, known for their developed sense of communication and imagination, do all the "EVOLVED" stuff for the survival of "ME" and consequently, what is "MINE". If you agree to this, even a little bit, you have answered my question. We are all hypocrites. Hypocrisy can be explained to be behaviour that contradicts what one claims to believe. Isn't that what we always do? What is convenient for us becomes "change" or "growth" or "evolution". What is not, becomes "hypocrisy". Simply because survival at the physical or mental level would require either exploiting something/one or need a change of your thought processes. This will result in multiple inconsistencies across your own actions. What is in your mind may not necessarily be your action. What is now your action may be different from what once was. And if you try to align everything, all the time, perhaps it may be the end of your survival. Not saying no one would have ever done that, but it will be rare. In some sense, probably they have truly evolved beyond the limitations of being human.

Hypocrisy has been one of my favourite topics to think about, note and at some level, practice. Not too proud of it though, but I realised it is embedded in my very nature as a human instinct. I said before that it is not too bitter a truth. I believe so, because tainting it as good or bad may be a result of your belief whether you are on the receiving end of it. Let me be clear, I am not preaching to do as Romans when in Rome. All I'm saying is, hypocrisy, just like humans, exists. Like hunger, thirst, temperature, air, water, earth and sun. It just is. Am I trying to justify, it? Doesn't matter. What exists needs no justification. Yet I find it funnily interesting to explore the ways of humans. With humans, I always feel that (I am not claiming to be an alien secretly shape-shifted to human form for a reconnaissance mission so that my fellows can invade):

Whatever I am or will be, after all, it is me,
The world around is mine and should be what I want it to be.

I don't despise humans, nor myself. My only attempt is to be more empathetic towards everything at large, recognising that the natural construct of survival has a much larger role to play than the fragile human imaginations about what humans are.

COLD

Cold,
It is cold.
The wind,
The weather,
The eyes, the heart,
Trying to find a flame,
A bit of warmth,
In the money and the food.
The wine and what they call mine.
In sex and beauty,
Or the satisfaction of doing their duty.
Maybe the body is warm,
But the blood cooled down long ago.
They don't feel; they think.
They are intelligent and practical.
They smoke, they have coffee.
Life is good as they see.
That's how it's supposed to be,
Like the beer they chug,
Cold.

THE HAIRDRESSERS

Yes, they have mirrors,
The hairdressers.
But then, today they showed me
Something more than just me.
They showed me what life is and what life could be.
Life is NOW, everywhere around.
All it takes is patience.
To realise that if you want to look good,
You must wait for your turn.
Bear some pain as life cuts through you,
Get rid of a part of you.
Holding your head high may not always be useful,
Obeying is not always slavery.
You will get all messed up in your own mess,
Looking all ugly and blotted.
You might not understand what's happening,
The end might be clear but the method, unknown.
Yet you embrace the possibilities
And trust the stranger with your neck,

Hoping for something to happen.
In the end, it pays, it always does,
Maybe the way you wanted, maybe not.
But better than what you were an hour ago.
How is life any different, I don't know.
All I know is that I saw it,
The meaning of life or the lack of it.
In my eyes, watching me from the mirror
Sitting across me,
At the place, we all call,
The Hairdressers.

POET

I came across this girl.
I told her I was sad,
A bit mad,
Treated a lad,
Somewhat bad.
But she smiled.
She seldom spoke,
Her eyes did the most.
She peeked into me,
Through my eyes that went hollow,
As hope left it long ago.
She mapped her way into my cold heart.
All it took was her breath,
To melt it down,
In which she dipped her magical pen,
And started writing on my soul,
A poem of love and hope and friendship and joy.
Life was no more gloomy or drab,
There was lustre in my eyes,
And music in my ears,
And that I had a right to laugh,
And share with her my tears,
That I was not so bad,
And there's nothing wrong with mad,
And even if I feel sad,

I would still be treated like a lad.
She wrote a poem,
That neither was a lie nor the truth,
But it made me meet myself,
Who was way beyond all of it.
Every moment I see her,
I wonder whether I can gather enough words,
To thank the girl who wrote bliss for me,
The girl who has many names,
But I know her as,
The poet.

LOST

They say you never value something,
Until it is lost.
Maybe they thought they had it in the first place.
That is the illusion, my friend,
That things start and come to an end.
These are the veils that give you pain,
That makes you feel that you lose and gain.
When thinking adds confusion and ignorance is easy,
It is a sign that you're lost.
When you think you belong to a pack,
It is a sign that you're lost.
When you think you found what you were looking for,
You're lost.
When you fight a battle with all your might
and think you are winning, you've really lost.
When you gain laughter over someone's pain,
You've actually lost.
When you start finding answers,
It's high time to realise that you're lost.
Life is not to be understood, to be gained or owned.
You may count your friends, both by blood and love.

You may count your knowledge, your intel, your emotions.
They were never yours to value or to devalue.
If you think you had any of it, you're lost.
Find your way o friend,
Even though that would mean you're lost.
You may not find sense in what I preach,
Yet, it is only a matter of time before it's true for each.
You don't have anything, and you will never have.
Because everything you think you had,
You have or will have,
Is nothing but LOST.

THE WORD

As again I try to rhyme,
And I repeat my crime,
Not so proud. I admit,
Yet feeling wiser at the end of wit.
Yes, I lied, I was a liar,
Yes, I lied. I was the liar.
My crime was neither big nor small,
I fell for something not worth the fall.
Greed makes you wish for both the milk and curd,
Just that it fails you from holding to your word.
What could have been a greater crime,
For, it's all about the word since the beginning time.
Every moment is about that word,
In speech and silence, it's all about that word.
Easy to give and easy to take,
Seldom true, more attractive to fake.
It is what a mother waits for since the birth,
And what teachers teach us without dearth.
It was the word on which she left her house,
It was the word that kept the lion from the mouse.
The word brought power to kings,
It was the word that gave children wings.

Yet I have the audacity to betray,
The nobility of every word I say.
Mates and souls, all awfully close,
Took my word as a fragrant rose.
For, like the devil, I had no horns,
I was cold enough to give them the thorns.
Even with the thorn did they give a smile,
And gaze at me calmly for a while.
These are who I betrayed for my thirst,
And beautify the lie that lies in my crust.
For a moment, it worked on me as well,
The truth from fiction even I wasn't able to tell.
They say crime never pays,
But something different, my experience says.
That which is paid is a lot of pain and loss,
As I see my peace go for a toss.
It is then that I realise that my word was a lie,
And I was foolishly proud as lie after lie passed by.
The light dawns, and the truth does appear,
For it was only the lie that caused fear.
Now, as I see, I'm alone in the midst of the herd,
All I had, have, and will have to stand by is the WORD.

BUT

There was something,
That had existed forever,
And perhaps will.
BUT –
You deserve freedom, BUT you need to comply.
You have a right to be yourself, BUT you cannot be shy.
Speak what you think, BUT don't offend me.
Honesty is the best policy, BUT sometimes you need some diplomacy.
Failures are stepping stones, BUT they don't fetch the value.
Justice is thy right, BUT only when you have the resources to sue.
Money can't buy happiness, BUT it is still good enough to sell your soul.
Looks don't matter, BUT that's how we value you.
Work and life should be balanced, BUT I need the file by tomorrow.
Friends are the true wealth, BUT I need to pay the rent.
Love is always loyal, BUT my body has needs.
God exists, BUT I can't see.

Maybe what I'm doing is wrong, BUT it is necessary.
The shield we hold to protect our hollow bodies,
Those who have lost everything, BUT flesh,
We crave to fill the void, created by our empty character,
BUT
We fail.

KEEP COUNTING

Keep counting.
Count the numbers, the pennies and time.
Count your steps as with your beats; they rhyme.
Perhaps counting is what we learn first,
And maybe it is what causes and quenches our thirst.
Though for some, it is a habit, bad,
That snatches joy and makes you sad.
I agree that counting may not always yield,
But for sure, it is a useful shield.
Counting makes you conscious and also aware.
Sometimes it's the only way to make you care.
Not about the things you have or could have had,
But about the deeds and the words you said.
Count the steps you still need to take,
A wonderful place if you aim to make.
Count those smiles, those satisfying sighs,
As your persistence touch new all-time highs.
Aim to account for those debts of sorrow,
That due to greed, the humans did borrow.
Account for those priceless wits and healthy hearts,
Which our vices are causing to depreciate in parts.

Counting does not solve problems by itself.
It just shows a mirror of the true self.
To change is a slow and steady thing,
Yet I'd say, keep counting.

JUSTIFICATION

There is a man that walks on the roads of every nation,
The one who has been witnessing his own cremation.
Where truth leads to dismal defamation,
And the slyest of cheaters are honoured with a coronation.
The so-called smart are the ones to get gratification,
And all this stupid fellow gets is justification.

The one who pays the last penny earns starvation,
The one who absconds billions earns the reputation.
The one who gifts her his heart gets mutilation,
The one who brings her lust gets a so-called Relation.
The one with money faces no hesitation,
And beggars with feelings just get justification.

NEVER BEG

Never beg.
It may sound good,
Ideal, words to live by,
But do you?
As every moment passes by,
You hope, you pray, you expect,
YOU BEG.
Yes, of course, you beg.
When fear preys on you,
Feeds on you -
Fear of losing your job, your people,
Fear of not getting what you want.
You WANT things to be your way,
You want, so you pray, you hope, you expect,
Expect people to be your way, the weather,
The stock markets, the restaurant queues to be
your way.
You think you WANT,
But all you do in your mind is BEG.
Free yourself,
Nothing was ever yours,
Things will always be what you never thought.
Don't beg for outcomes, things, people, feelings,
respect.
If you think I'm a loser,

That's fine with me.
Wait till I come all guns blazing,
Even after which I may win, may lose.
But do you know what, I still don't care.
'Coz I don't want to hope or expect victory,
I don't want to BEG,
So shouldn't you,
Never, ever.

SO WHAT?

Two words, one question.
A thousand meanings, if you pay attention.
Two words that bring you the light,
Purging all the filters in your sight.
Try testing your strength and ask,
Facing the truth can be a task.
When life seems dim and grim,
Ask yourself SO WHAT?

If you are the one who falls hundred times,
And you fall victim to all those crimes,
Don't let it stop you from moving ahead,
Don't let it get into your head,
When life gifts you the best,
And you seem to be better than the rest,
Ask yourself SO WHAT?

Your height is just a lie your ego tells you,
Try looking to the stars shining high above you.
Don't let it stop you from moving ahead,
Don't let it get into your head,
Life isn't good or bad, happy, or sad,
Your ego uses these stories to drive you mad.
In victory or defeat, ask yourself SO WHAT?

CAPTAIN

You are the captain of your life,
Are you?
Are you driving your ship?
Is it something else?
It doesn't matter,
'Coz driving your ship makes you a driver,
Not a captain.

A captain is not the one
Who knows how to repair his broken engine,
Not necessarily one who knows how to load a turret.
A captain is the one who takes responsibility,
Of oneself and all.
Agrees to go in the middle of nowhere,
For years together,
To seek an unknown enemy,
Every moment he runs the risk,
Of being killed, captured, or drowned.
Yet he stays,
As the sole shield between the death and the team,
Freedom, country, and hope.

Do you accept responsibility for what happens?

Are you afraid of failure?
Can you look yourself in the eye?
When you lose someone because of you?
You know the answer,
You know who you are,
The question is,
Whether you really want to rise
And become someone more than a hypocrite
Or a person with courage, speed, intelligence,
and character,
A captain.

I CAN

I want to rise,
Beyond the veil of my vision,
Above the heights of irony,
And below the depths of misery.
I can smell this world,
As I taste it, sip by sip,
Making me high,
As my tears run dry.

I adjust to the seasons,
Maybe that is how I Fall,
Into the abyss of indulgence,
Opening my senses to the truth,
Or lack of it.
That being a treacherous whore
Who sells character for cakes,
Is no different than the bard
Who gets richer for every story he bakes.

This cake is tasty, delicious, and tempting.
The cake of world, man, and God.
The cake of my lust and greed,
Stored in the castle of my vanity,
Guarded by the corpses of my relationships,
As I enslave my loved ones,

In the garb of my manipulative hunger.

For the cake, my cake,
Crushing people, lives, and truth and lies,
Because I have made the God and the Satan,
Whatever I want is what God wants me to have,
Whatever I snatch from you is what Satan made you lose,
Not because I must,
Or I like it,
Or it's the right thing to do,
But simply because,
I'm intoxicated enough to realise,
I can.

DONE FOR THE DAY

Yes, I smiled.
Yes, I cried.
For the moments I lived today,
A few ages I died.
I don't know what else to say,
I'm just done for the day.

Yes, the day was long,
Not a very melodious song.
I treaded and toiled,
As my heart and soul soiled.
With malice, lust, relief, and glee,
Another bit of myself crumble, I see.

I am the devil and, the God as you say,
With one I kill while with other I pray,
I'm just done with it, done for the day.
I have loved and betrayed,
I spoke the truth when I lied.
Relieved I am, as my principles for sale I lay,
Since I got my coins for my character,
I am done for the day.

YOU CANNOT ERASE ME

A random walk by a house full of books,
Full of people with cold faces and dull looks,
A book with a title very inspiring I see,
In black and bold, it said, 'You cannot erase me!".
Apparently inspiring, but then I gave some thought,
I happen to think about what
it means and what it does not.
I realised what I used to preach back since long,
I am a story, a poem, a play, a song.
I am a memory that pricks you,
That may bore you, give you pain,
Make you smile and laugh and think you read me in vain.
I am not a verse written on parchment,
I am a proverb sculpted in stone.
It took pain and dust and disgust of many,
I'm not a beautiful story or a romantic one,
It's not a pleasant one or one where the rags turn to riches,

The hero doesn't win always; the villain is not always bad.
It's not good, nor bad, neither right nor wrong,
But it's damn sure a true one.
You can read me, ignore me, despise me,
'You cannot erase me!'

THE LADDER TO GOODNESS

Work hard, they say,
They say, do good,
Good things are difficult,
Difficult to understand; difficult to do,
Doing takes perseverance,
Perseverance takes a toll,
The toll on my body,
The body that strives and falls,
Falls on the snowy weightless sheet,
A sheet which is flat and down,
Down below the crystal ball of light,
The light that shows how dark it is,
Dark is my mind and my heart and my soul,
The soul that is said to continue,
Continue the struggle and life and death,
Death of the conscience and the right and wrong,
Wrong was the man and the woman with the apple,
Apple fell just once, but humans still fall,
Fall into the abyss of the past,
Past of the flowers and the birds and trees,
Trees of knowledge, pride, and wealth,

Wealth like coins that can buy misery,
The misery of the selfish self that craves,
Craves for money, might and matter,
The matter is the future, but the future doesn't matter,
The matter was the past, yet past is all that matters,
Matters in the present still don't matter,
All that matters is the story,
The story where I win,
Win the people, money, and power,
Power to see and change the future,
Future that I see in my crystal ball,
The crystal ball that lies up above the sheet,
The sheet on which my body lies,
My body, tired of the fear and good,
Good, that is good for all,
But I need to work hard, they say,
They say, do good.

THE GIRL WITH BOBBELLY (STRAWBERRY) EYES

Change is the only constant they say,
And every change is as fragile as clay.
Change changes whatever you know to be true.
But the change is here to stay.
Some changes I like, some I don't,
The ones I like, I write,
The ones I don't, probably I won't.
One of my favourite changes was a person I met,
From whom, a lot of love, care, and warmth I get.
I'm not selfish enough to love her only for that,
Though she does pamper me as a spoiled brat.
Coming back to the moment I met her,
I knew there was something unique about her.
The firm smile that could last a mile,
Her pinky dress and her pinkier vibe,
I was relieved to know her taste for fries,

But what caught me completely; were her
Bobbelly eyes.
She likes to share food but not the last bite,
A grain of dust is sure to give her a fright.
She loves dogs, the moon, and stars,
And she uses her pen to decorate her scars.
From sappy cuddly romcoms to the deadly
sinister spies,
All stories are good if you see them through her
Bobbelly eyes.

It is not that we only laugh all time,
To lie about that would be a heinous crime.
We also did have our own share of tears,
But it becomes easy when we hold each other in
our fears.
Music is a healer when she plays it or sings,
For some reason, she gets shy when the doorbell
rings.
She says she does not look good,
And that she needs to cut down on food.
I get very conscious due to her healthy
inspirations,
And a few moments later, we are hogging on our
temptations.
We now never feel guilty for food,
And about the looks, I feel she's been rude,
Rude to herself and her beautiful being,
As she does not observe and is only seeing,

Seeing through the dogmas and the notions of the wretched world,
In falsehood and greed, it has already twirled,
Life, as I see it, is beautiful, and so is she.
Because I do observe and not just see,
Because I see her and myself and my life,
My friend, philosopher, guide, and wife,
Into the free, light, and hopeful skies,
Happiness and glee through her Bobbelly eyes.

THE DISTANT FRIEND

Being introvert is not that great,
Very few love you, while most hate,
Of those few, some stick till the end,
The one who I know to be my distant friend.

My earliest memory of her is below a tree,
When innocence was bliss and thoughts were free.
She came near me, jumping down the bark,
Her eyes like pearls and her fur a little dark.
Her timid, trembling ears made her look cute
As I interfered in her feast with the fruit.
While exchanging a glance, a lovely message did she send,
I never hoped a squirrel to be my new distant friend.

Playing games was not my thing,
Occasionally, just a slide or a swing.
Not that I disliked others,
Maybe I realised no one bothers.
With toffees, a glass of water, and a book,

With these, to the window, myself I hook.
There I see my darling crush,
She was indeed in some rush.
Tweaking her delicate neck around,
Her gracious tail kept off the ground.
A glance and off she went, that was the end,
But I was happy to see my distant friend.

She didn't frequent my thoughts, my ground,
Nor was I attached, strong, and profound.
But as you grow up or at least try to,
You find new reasons to cry to.
Solace, I found in a deserted park,
Where silence rejoiced while feelings left a mark.
Out of the blue, she was there
Not near but in the rear.
A few nibbles, and smirks and she goes
Behind the bushes of fragrant rose.
Not that she did care,
Nothing could I share.
Yet I choose to believe
I was a reason to be there.

Often its assurance is what you need,
Of grim pages of life when you read.
Intent be different, the desired result I got,
It made me calm while others could not.
Ripples of joy did she send,

Unknowingly, she played my distant friend.

Still, as I pave my way through the forest,
Cement, brick, and wires, among the rest.
Smiles are fake, and friends are still few,
They all seek the same; only words are new.
The picture looks cool
With high walls, green lawns, and clothes,
beautiful.
Yet, in the depth of shine,
Nothing seems fine.
Stakes and fakes are all high.
You kill yourself and heave a sigh.
Amidst the beeps, weeps. And creeps,
There is still someone taking joyful leaps.
The one who jumps and minds oneself
Reminds me of the importance to love myself.
Maybe they don't love; they don't care.
That doesn't make my hatred fair.
Her glance soothes me,
Though I know it's not me that she sees.
Inspiration is enough to light the spark,
One that can destroy the dark.
That is what she gifts me every day,
Even if both of us have nothing to say.
She still makes a point to appear at the end.
Though ignorant, I love my distant friend.

DROPS OF DEW

Stories describe people, if they may,
Some adventurous while some as dry as hay.
To summarize my life, I need words only a few,
It all started and remained between the drops of dew.

Unhappy I was to be born; I don't know why,
What other inference do you draw from the fact that I did cry?
Yet, as moments passed by,
A heave of relief, I sighed.
There was the divine looking to the boy born new,
Those love-filled eyes looked me through the drops of dew.

For some, it was the birth of a generation,
For some, a reason of celebration.
It was only one on earth who herself was born again,
Like a butterfly from the cocoon as her wings, she trained.
This evolution was for taking me into her realm,
With that, I felt all the love and calm.

As the warmth of her affection greeted a life new,
Within the protection of her wings,
All I could see were the shining drops of dew.

Life does not stop; I came to know,
It was time to sit in a school row.
I know I did not cry for sure,
With her love, it was not that difficult to endure.
While my eyes turned to her for one last time before I stepped in,
She gave me that push and assured me I would win.
It didn't seem easy to let a part of your heart to some people new,
With fear and optimism, she looked at me through the drops of dew.

To excel was always her teaching to me,
I tried to be her as much as I could, that worked for me.
If I were to win in all the tests,
It was due to her courage apart from the rest.
While some doubted it, some greeted.
Some gave me a standing ovation, while some remained seated.
It is only her whose happiness knew no bounds,
As my name was announced rounds after rounds.

With head held high and expressions few,
All she did was smile through the drops of dew.

As life moved ahead,
Through invigorating experiences did I tread.
It was to turn only worse, it seemed,
I was useless to many, it deemed.
Dead, I became as my dreams shattered,
To most of them, it didn't matter.
Failure was not the worst pain,
It was worse than death to let her hope to go in vain.
The lesson that I learnt with a heavy cost,
It is the cheater who loses more than the one whose trust is lost.
Still, she chose to forgive,
And taught me to look forward as I live.
She embraced me with my failures while speaking words few,
Belief stayed in her eyes with the drops of dew.

As life gets weird and hard to deal,
The scars only increase and do not heal.
Frustration and anger start to take over,
When pressure is high, and morale is lower.
We do fight over things wrong and right,
But never, it is a question of might.
While some we conclude, many we do not,
Sometimes just blabbering at the other, a lot.

While we share our joys and sorrows,
Sometimes it takes one look to understand
What lies in the burrows.
To share ourselves, we need words only a few,
As we see each other through the drops of dew.

Though this appears to be a long account,
There are uncountable things I just cannot count.
As she bore decades of scars and bruises,
She endured even the darkest of the times
Some wins, some losses.
I'm not sure where she gets her strength from,
But I'm sure that she is who I get my strength
from.
Life shall be daunting, and hard for sure,
While we defeat many of the enemies,
For some, there may not be a cure.
What is necessary is the spirit to hold the
ground,
To hold that, the inspirations are very few,
But what keeps me going are the drops of dew.

www.ingramcontent.com/pod-product-compliance
Lightning Source LLC
Chambersburg PA
CBHW051743130826
49812CB00033B/975
9789357445603